a book about girls, their rights, and their voice

girl power

in the family

by Karen Lound

Lerner Publications Company • Minneapolis

Lerner Publications Company
A Division of Lerner Publishing Group
241 First Avenue North
Minneapolis, MN 55401 U.S.A.

Website address: www.lernerbooks.com

The publisher thanks Kazuko, Lara, and Sara Collins, who were photographed for the cover of this book.

Library of Congress Cataloging-in-Publication Data

Lound, Karen.
   Girl power in the family : a book about girls, their rights, and their voice / by Karen Lound.
      p.   cm.
   Includes bibliographical references.
   Summary: Discusses the relationships between girls and their families, the gender issues that affect these relationships, and ways girls can develop their own identities.
   ISBN 0–8225–2692–1 (lib. bdg. : alk. paper)
   1. Teenage girls—Family relationships—Juvenile literature.
   2. Girls—Life skills guides—Juvenile literature. 3. Self-esteem in adolescence—Juvenile literature. [1. Teenage girls. 2. Sex role.
   3. Self-actualization (Psychology). 4. Family life.] I. Title.
   HQ755.85.L69   2000
   306.874—dc21   99–38096

Manufactured in the United States of America
1 2 3 4 5 6 – JR – 05 04 03 02 01 00

Contents

Family Matters

Sometimes it seems like growing up in itself is a very hard thing to do, and being a girl adds more complexity.

—Jessica, 16

How do you feel about growing up? About being a girl in your family? Here's a story from Jessica, 14 (a different Jessica than the one quoted above).

"Last summer my best friend and I were running up and down the halls in a hotel, stealing soap and food supplies out of the housekeeping carts, spitting out of the windows, taking ice cubes from the ice machines and leaving them on the floor to let them melt. My parents found out, and we got in trouble. They said that what we did was 'rude and unladylike.'

"Then, at Thanksgiving, my boy cousins did the same thing. The adults just said, 'Boys will be boys'! I told my parents that I knew I shouldn't have done what I had done, but they had a double standard. If I got in trouble, the boys should have gotten in trouble, too.

"I reacted the way I did," says Jessica, "because I knew it wasn't fair that my friend and I got in trouble for the same exact thing the boys got away with. I felt absolutely awful when this happened. Girls have urges to get their adrenaline rushing, too!"

> *It wasn't fair that my friend and I got in trouble for the same exact thing the boys got away with.*
>
> —Jessica, 14

Great Expectations

Has anything like that ever happened to you? Has it ever seemed that your parents used one set of rules for boys and another for girls? Do adults in your family appear to have certain expectations for you because you're a girl? When people expect that a girl should act in a certain way just because she is a girl, the expectation is known as a gender expectation.

Expectations aren't necessarily bad. They can be good or bad or a mix. Let's say your parents expect you to help out around the house. This is just a part of everyday life in many households. But if you are the only girl in a family of four brothers and you have to clean the house on weekends while your brothers have free time, that may be a rule based on a gender bias. A gender bias is a gender expectation that turns out to be limiting or unfair.

A gender bias or a gender expectation isn't necessarily meant to hurt a girl! Parents don't

A Mixed Bag

Gender expectations—being expected to act in a certain way because you're a girl—can be a mix of good and bad. Here are some of the gender expectations that some people may have for girls.

- girls will help with housework
- being pretty is important to girls
- girls are often silly or illogical
- girls are safest at home

usually think of their expectations as limiting their children. Expectations and even biases in a family are probably intended to work for a girl's best interest.

Most often, parents see their rules as being just the way things have always been done. Gender expectations and gender biases are based on opinions that have been around for a long time, a fact that makes them hard to notice. The example about a girl cleaning the house while her brothers have free time is an extreme example. Lots of times, gender bias is more subtle—harder to see.

All the Differences

Families are like the stars in the night sky. Each is different. Think about the families you know. Do some of your friends have lots of brothers or sisters? Or none? Do some of them live with both a mom and a dad, while others live with just one parent?

Some differences, such as religion, can have a big effect on families. Life in a Muslim family may be quite different from life in a Jewish, Christian, or nonreligious family.

Ethnicity is still another important difference. According to experts Charles H. Mindel and Robert Habenstein, "ethnicity" refers to traditions passed down from one generation to the next. A

Greek family that has just come to the United States may have many ethnic traditions that are distinct from those in an Irish-American family.

Personalities and personal style play a role. Some families are loud; some are quiet. Some are always on the go; some mostly stay home. Education, the size of a family, and the ages of family members are other differences, as well as where people live, what the parents do to earn a living, and how much money the family has.

The list goes on. Obviously, there's no end to what the word *family* might mean to any one girl. Expectations—including gender expectations—are bound to be different from family to family. You'll want to consider all the many things that make your family unique as you consider your family's expectations for you.

No one kind of family is the "right" kind. But every family is important. Understanding your family can make life a lot easier. Your family can be the source of your values and sense of belonging, a source of security and strength. A family can support a girl's sense of her true self.

A Mix of Feelings

Recent studies have shown that girls feel pressure to turn away from their true selves as they become teenagers. Yet in a girl's teen years, she needs her "self" more than ever! Understanding how you fit in your family can help you understand who you are. Knowing who you are—having a strong sense of self—will help you make good decisions about your life.

It's natural to have a mix of feelings about your family and yourself, especially in the years when girls are changing so fast. Many girls find that, as they grow up, they need their families more than ever. But girls need to feel independent, too! Sometimes that makes it hard to talk to family members and to feel understood by them.

Here's what Jessica (the sixteen-year-old Jessica) found. "When I started junior high, I wanted to be independent. That was a very frustrating time for me," she remembers. "Everything I said or did seemed to contradict what my parents seemed to think. . . . I wanted so badly to be different, to not be connected [to my family], to have my own identity without their opinions mattering." Not surprisingly, Jessica and her family drifted apart.

> *I* wanted so badly to be different . . . to have my own identity without [my family's] opinions mattering.
>
> —Jessica, 16

Slowly, Jessica began to realize that she wanted to be herself, but she also needed her family. "Now I realize that their opinion of me does matter," she says. "They will be there for me when no one else is. I am connected to them. I'm glad I realize that now before too much time was lost."

A girl from Maryland, Miranda, 14, wrote a poem called "Blue" about her mixture of feelings about herself and her family. In the poem, the color blue meant withdrawn and sad feelings. But, to Miranda, blue also stood for the peaceful feeling of being close to someone. As Miranda put it: "Blue is the feeling of my mom holding me tight; it is the color of her saying it will be all right, of us talking in the moonlight. Blue is the color of her saying good night."

Miranda's poem reflects courage. She takes the risk and describes what she feels. Her mother is there with her, offering support—maybe even on days when she faces her own sad feelings.

Girl Talk

In writing this book, I got input from lots of girls. Some girls talked about how families can affect a girl's career decisions, friendships, dating, schoolwork, participation in sports, and more. Many girls shared ideas for how to cope with the

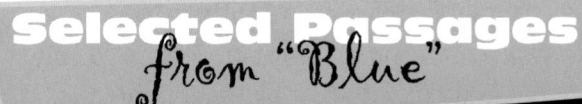

Selected Passages from "Blue"

B lue is the feeling of my mom holding
me tight,
It is the color of her saying it
will be all right,
of us talking in the moonlight.
Blue is the color of her saying good night.

Blue is like a good night kiss after
a date,
Blue is the bang of firecrackers set
in my ears,
Blue is the color of running away
because of my fears.

—Miranda, 14

conflicting feelings that so often come with families. Others offered advice on how to talk to a parent, get along with a sibling (brother or sister), or "blend" in a blended family.

Many girls talked about gender expectations in their families. Some noticed that families—and girls themselves—have different expectations. As you hear from girls in the pages to come, you may get some new insights into your family. There are lots of great comments here!

But ultimately, this book is about you. It's about becoming strong and confident. In a way, it's about holding onto your true self. That doesn't mean rejecting your family! In fact, sometimes, it can mean accepting your family at the same time that you accept yourself. Addressing expectations and biases around you, whether in your family or anywhere else, is a part of that process.

> *It's just nice to know that ... other girls are going through the same things.*
>
> **—Meg, 13**

I hope that, as you read along, you'll hear your own voice and the voices of other true selves. You'll find some strategies—and support—for becoming the kind of girl you want to be, in your family and on your own.

chapter two

The Birth of Bias

> Society has expected us [girls] to be perfect. I don't understand it. I don't think anybody really does.
>
> —*Emily*, 15

Where do expectations and biases come from? Why do parents sometimes seem to treat daughters differently than they treat sons?

Remember the old nursery rhyme "Sugar and spice and everything nice, that's what little girls are made of"? To write her book *The Difference*, Judy Mann met with a group of women at a conference and asked them what expectations they had for girls. The group came up with a number of words to describe girls, including *sugar and spice, princess, sweet, kind, a leader but not flamboyant, quiet, ladylike, loving, strong within the family, modest outside the family.*

You may feel that many of these qualities aren't all bad. What's wrong with being sweet and quiet and ladylike? Nothing, as long as you feel free to be everything else a girl might be: *assertive, strong, someone who speaks her mind, baseball player*, and so on.

The words we use to describe ourselves and one another have power, says Judy Mann. "What we don't understand very well," she wrote, "is . . . how deeply ingrained our own ideas of what is appropriate female and male behavior have become." In other words, parents often deeply believe certain things to be true of boys and other things to be true of girls. They may have these expectations from the day a child is born. Parents "stamp those beliefs on babies from the moment we learn their gender," says Mann.

> *My dad often told me to be quiet. . . . I tried to be better by not talking at all, and I grew up to be a very shy girl.*
>
> —Lisa, 16

Nature versus *Nurture*

Why does it sometimes seem a girl is "supposed" to have certain qualities? Why can't a girl just be herself?

Researchers have tried to find out where gender expectations come from. Two ideas, or theories, have to do with "nature" and "nurture." The nature theory says we're born with certain qualities. We inherit them from our parents, grandparents, and other ancestors. The color of our eyes is an inherited trait. A beautiful singing voice may be an inherited trait.

Why can't a girl just be herself?

What happens if people believe some skills are inborn—meaning they are present the moment a person is born? Consider a mom who believes her son has more inborn logic than her daughter has. She also believes that reading a map is a task that requires logic. Will she ask her son to read the map on family road trips? Or will she ask her daughter?

Related to the nature theory is the idea that gender expectations came about because of biology. Females give birth—that's part of a woman's biology. Gradually, because women had the babies, they came to be seen as the parent who would stay close to home and take care of the babies. Men—more typically the providers of food—were more free to go wherever they needed to go.

The second theory is the nurture theory. It focuses on the world around us. A child's family, community, and nation are part of the world around that child. The child may go to a good school, to a poor school, or to no school. Each child lives in a different environment, which nurtures certain traits in that child.

Consider a child in a large family that talks constantly together. This child may learn to talk a lot, or he or she may grow quiet, finding it hard to speak up amid all the other people talking. Either way, the child's environment has nurtured a certain trait.

Culture is a part of anyone's environment. Culture is the typical behavior of a group of people. The group's culture is their way of life, ideas, customs, and traditions. Anthropologist Charlotte J. Frisbie says culture decides how people are treated and shapes gender expectations. Culture influences how females and males are expected to act.

Gao, 13, belongs to a Hmong family that recently immigrated to the United States. "Hmong culture is hard on girls," she says. "Hmong culture says girls shouldn't go out and have fun with their friends. They should stay home and wash dishes and help their mom. Guys can go out and do whatever they want."

Is that good or bad? Pam, 14, is also a member

of the Hmong community in America. She says, "In Hmong culture, the family sort of forces you to grow up faster."

Another girl, Alisa, 15, lives in South Carolina. Her parents are wealthy and prominent in their community. Alisa is part of a culture that expects that girls will be debutantes at about age eighteen. A debutante is introduced to adult society at a "coming-out" ball. When Alisa was fourteen, her parents expected her to take ballroom dancing lessons to prepare for her coming-out ball. That was a problem for Alisa, who wanted to participate in track and field instead.

Many researchers don't agree with either the nature theory or the nurture theory. J. David Smith, an expert on twin psychology, says the nature versus nurture argument is too limited. Growing up involves more than "just genes or the environment," as he puts it. "People are actively involved in creating their own personalities," he says. "They make different choices, choose different directions."

The Perfect Girl

What should a girl be like in modern times? To get the clearest answer, I asked girls to describe the "perfect" girl.

> *The perfect girl would be very happy, smart, kind to people. This girl would be liked by everyone.*
>
> —Kasie, 13

"The perfect girl would be very happy, smart, kind to people," said Kasie, 13, from Minnesota. "This girl would be liked by everyone."

"When I picture a perfect girl," wrote Emily, 15, "I see someone who is always ready, always giving, and always kind. She is organized and punctual."

"The perfect girl would be pretty, popular, have perfect teeth, have money and a boyfriend," said Miranda, 14.

When Nicole, 11, of Minnesota thought of the perfect girl, she thought of looks. "I have this picture in my mind of what I'd look like if I were perfect," said Nicole. "I wouldn't be flat-chested like I am, and I would be pretty and tall because I'm almost a runt."

Lisa, 16, from California, said the perfect girl would be "popular." She would also "get good grades without seeming to even try."

Of course, the perfect girl is an ideal, not real. But sometimes family members and other people seem to expect real girls to be perfect girls. Lisa said, "Almost everybody wants me to act a certain way. Teachers want me to be studious and raise my hand constantly in class. Friends want me to

More about the Perfect Girl

I try so hard to be like the perfect girl. The perfect girl would be very happy, smart, kind to people. This girl would be liked by everyone. [She] could be fat, skinny, ugly, or beautiful; to me, it doesn't matter what she looks like, as long as she is happy with who she is. I don't know anyone who is truly that pure and perfect.

The perfect girl has lots of friends—true friends—and can get through the day without questioning who loves her and if she is good enough for anyone. I am unlike her in that I am always wondering if people truly do care for me. No one should have to ask those questions, but at times it is so hard not to.

—Kasie, 13

be social and hang out with them all the time. They don't like it when I go off to chess club during lunch instead of staying with them."

Not Necessarily

Not every girl wants to be the perfect girl, though. "My mom is perfect," writes Alicia, 13, of Texas. "She is nice and you can say, pretty. I like her because she helps me a lot with many things. I don't want to be like her because we are two different persons, although she is my mother."

"I don't think I would want to be perfect," says Lisa. "Everyone would expect me to stay perfect, and I would want to do things like just hanging out at home watching TV or reading or talking on the phone, while the perfect girl would always be doing something, and she would have no time to herself."

> I feel better about my looks when I'm around my family.
>
> —Evelyn, 14

"I'm afraid of being her [the perfect girl] in some ways," writes Emily. "No one, in my perception, is perfect. We have to realize that everyone makes mistakes, that we are our own person."

"I don't feel I have to be a perfect girl," says Erin, 9. "I don't really mind what people say about me. You

don't have to be perfect. You can just be yourself."
This is good advice to keep in mind when you feel
pressure from parents, teachers, or other adults to
be a certain kind of girl.

The Confidence Gap

Why can't a girl always be totally herself? We
can't say with certainty exactly where any one
gender expectation comes from, whether it's our
own expectation or someone else's. We do know
every girl needs the freedom to be herself. As one
psychologist, Alex J. Packer, says, a person's talent
and inclination—the things she likes to do—should
determine her role, not her gender.

Judy Mann asked her conference group to come
up with words describing how either a boy or a
girl might be expected to act. These included
*confident, motivated, honest, problem solver,
responsible, sensitive, curious, active,* and many
others. It's okay to want to be *pretty* or *nice,* to
want to be a mother. But you can be these things
and also be *messy* or *spunky.* You could work as a
plumber or *firefighter.* You could not be a mother.

Researchers who believe in the nurture theory
say that some parents and other adults condition,
or train, girls to be sweet, nice, and so on. Jeanne
Elium and Don Elium, authors of a book called
Raising a Daughter, say parents may reward a girl

when she's sweet and nice and punish her when she's spunky or aggressive. When a father says, "Be a good girl and help Mom cook dinner," he is promising a reward. The reward is that he will think of his daughter as a "good girl" if she acts a certain way. Many parents don't stop to think about this kind of conditioning.

Think again about the example of a mom asking her son to read the map on family road trips. The more often the son reads the map, the more his map-reading skills will likely grow. The mom is conditioning her son and helping him develop skills. She's helping to make her own expectations come true.

Peggy Orenstein, author of a book called *SchoolGirls: Young Women, Self-Esteem, and the Confidence Gap,* says more and more parents are noticing their own gender biases. Instead of assuming girls are bad at math and boys are bad at reading, more parents are encouraging both girls and boys in both areas. Teachers see the results in standardized test scores. Each year, the "gender gap" in test scores gets smaller. Boys and girls are scoring more and more alike.

A gap still remains, however, according to Orenstein. She calls it a "confidence gap." As many girls reach adolescence, they have less confidence than boys have. They don't believe in themselves as strongly.

The skills girls—or boys—have are important. But what girls and boys *believe* about their skills—and themselves—is important, too. No matter the biases that exist around a girl, problems start when she begins to believe a bias herself. If people around a girl think she's *illogical,* after a while she may agree. A girl with this belief about herself could grow up to fear logical tasks—like becoming an engineer. A girl who loses confidence may limit her options.

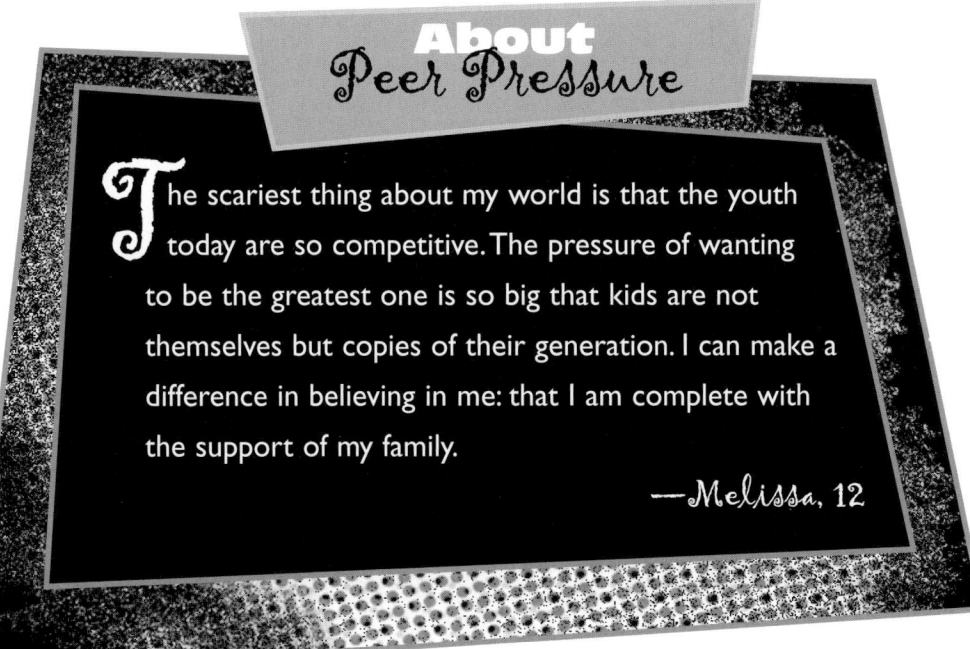

About Peer Pressure

The scariest thing about my world is that the youth today are so competitive. The pressure of wanting to be the greatest one is so big that kids are not themselves but copies of their generation. I can make a difference in believing in me: that I am complete with the support of my family.

—Melissa, 12

A Confident Voice

> **My family doesn't pressure me to look skinny and pretty. I pressure myself.**
> —Liliana, 12

The messages about what a girl "should" be are harder and harder to escape as a girl grows up. Even girls who do not get these messages from their families get them from the media—magazines, music, movies, TV, and the like.

Many studies have been done about the media and girls' looks. These studies offer a good example of the way we get messages, often without realizing it, about gender expectations. Most models and actresses shown in the media are considered beautiful. Most have slim bodies. Because the media is all around us, the "thin" look is all around us. Many girls get the message that being beautiful means being thin. In fact, many girls never feel slim enough! (Ever hear a friend say, "Oh, I'm so fat!" or "I'm dieting"?)

Mimi Nichter, Mark Nichter, and Sheila Parker are anthropologists who studied the effect of the media on girls. White girls were more affected by media messages than black girls are, they found. More often, black girls believed that "looking good" means how a girl moves, how she thinks, and how confident she feels. Black girls found these qualities not in the media but in their families. "Black girls told us their mothers and grandmothers are beautiful," said Mimi Nichter. "That's an outrageous thought for white girls."

The more you feel you are what you "should" be, the more confidence you have. The more you feel you are not what you "should" be, the more you may lose confidence. You can end up feeling bad or abnormal. You can't develop your own strength and power if you think you are bad or abnormal.

Just as the media teaches girls that girls "should" be thin, parents and other adults often teach that girls "should" be nice, quiet, and ladylike. Mary Pipher, author of *Reviving Ophelia: Saving the Selves of Adolescent Girls,* says these messages keep girls from being what she calls "authentic." Being authentic means being true to yourself and all the many ways you might feel, act, or think. The more you can be authentic, the stronger your inner voice becomes. The stronger your inner voice, the more you can turn to yourself for answers in troubled times.

Looks are pretty unimportant when you step out of magazine and TV land.

—Reanna, 14

chapter three

The Making of Relationships

We exist in a web of relationships.

—*Lyn Mikel Brown and Carol Gilligan*

How are you at relationships? Get along great with everybody all the time? If your answer is no, join the crowd. Most girls experience ups and downs in relationships.

Here's how Emily feels. "I think society puts pressure on girls in relationships more than [society pressures] boys," she says. "It seems that if guys are mad at each other, they don't really need a reason. They make up sooner, without talking about it. Girls, on the other hand, usually have to have a reason to do anything involving relationships."

Relationships can be complicated! At the same time, for most girls, relationships are especially important, according to some experts on girls' psychology. As Jeanne Elium and Don Elium put it, "Girls define themselves and their world by the state of their relationships."

Lisa talks about the way she viewed her relationship with her father and how that view contributed to her definition of herself. "My dad loved to play around with my little brother," she says. "They would wrestle, and Dad would give him piggyback rides and such.

"Unfortunately, Dad didn't like me to be around as much. He never played with me, and he often told me to be quiet if I was talking. I tried to be better by not talking at all, and I grew up to be a very shy girl."

Remember how we talked about expectations that girls will be *quiet, well behaved, ladylike,* and *nice?* Relationships can be pretty tricky for anybody, anytime. But these expectations can make relationships even trickier for girls. As girls grow up and go through their teen years, the going can get especially rough.

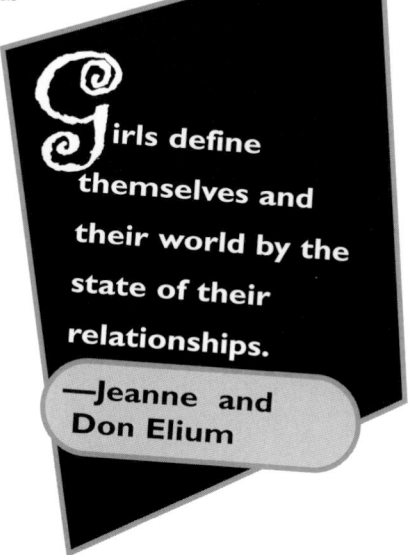

Girls define themselves and their world by the state of their relationships.

—Jeanne and Don Elium

Going Underground
with Feelings

Lyn Mikel Brown and Carol Gilligan, two researchers, have studied many girls' issues. According to their studies, as girls approach adolescence, it's harder for them to speak their minds.

A girl may feel it's too risky to say what she means and feels. Girls may fear being left without friends or being disapproved of by family members. "I'm scared of rejection," writes Miranda. "Most people are. I'm also scared of not being liked or of getting a bad reputation."

When the risks are too great, a girl may go "underground" with her feelings. Tess, 13, did that after her older sister, Dali, died. "My mother felt an amazing amount of grief," Tess explains. "My brothers reacted in their own ways, each going into their worlds." Although no one pressured Tess to act a certain way, she still felt it became her job to look after her mother.

Often, that meant Tess didn't allow herself to express her own feelings. "I lapsed into my own despair and sadness only when there was no one around," she writes. The risks involved in venting her own feelings were too great. If Tess leaned on other people, she feared everyone would collapse. As Tess put it, "I became the rock to keep the family sane."

In the end, the real Tess was buried. "Many people, friends included, think I'm a lot stronger than I actually am," she says. "They think I can cope with anything, when I'd really like to break down and cry."

Tess says she and her mom and Dali had been feminists before Dali died. "My family never pressured me to fit the stereotype for a girl before," according to Tess. But in putting her family before herself, Tess felt "cast into the role of a stereo-typed girl." Holding her family together was the "perfect" thing for Tess to do.

It's hard to sort out the difficult feelings related to a death and the things that may happen because a person is a girl. It seemed to Tess that her experience was influenced by her gender. "This didn't happen in the same way for my brothers," she reports.

> **G**irls seem to have so many more emotions than boys, and they deal with them differently.
> —Jessica, 16

What's the Use?

Situations may happen again and again in your family where no one hears you or listens to your side of the story. This is another reason girls become quiet. They give up.

This can happen especially when a girl shows anger and frustration. "I argued a lot for a couple of years, and it's really hard because I know it doesn't really do anything," says Pam, 14. "So now I try not to argue because it doesn't really make any difference. It doesn't change anything—they don't listen."

"I'm not allowed to say what I want to say," says Erin. "If I say that kind of stuff, I might get grounded. So I don't speak out. I just don't say anything."

Nicole, 11, sometimes feels the same way. "Everyone always babies my little sister," she says. "I get no attention except from my friends. So it's sort of hard to communicate with my family because they're busy worrying about my sister. I just don't talk to them hardly anymore. I just get silent. I kind of don't care anymore if I don't get any attention."

> I'm not allowed to say what I want to say.
>
> —Erin, 9

TWO Yous

Brown and Gilligan also talk about girls developing two selves—the private self and the public self. The public self is the person who is

Who I Am Scrapbook

*S*ometimes girls feel that, no matter what they do, they can't budge their families on important issues. What then?

One thing that can help is a scrapbook to remind you of who you are. Gather anything you love that can be pasted on paper—ticket stubs to that great concert, a blue ribbon for a science fair project, a note from your best friend, that drawing you made of your cat, photographs of yourself and people who care about you. If you don't have a blank book or scrapbook, just use plain paper and tie the pages together with a ribbon.

Keep adding to your scrapbook. Then each time you pull it out, you'll see the "real" you—the girl who's growing inside and out—shining from the pages.

acceptable to other people. Another self, the private self, is honest.

The public self is afraid of what will happen if the truth is spoken. So the public self is silent a lot. It gives up when parents make up their minds. There's no use in talking things over, even if they're wrong. Or at least that's what the public self believes.

As the public self gives up in favor of parents, friends, or others who have control over her, write Brown and Gilligan, the private self starts to feel smaller and smaller. Soon it's hard to hear what the private self has to say. A girl has to struggle to know what her private self thinks or believes or feels. A girl at this stage is in danger of losing her private self.

At a Crossroads

A girl who has trouble hearing her private self is at an important crossroads, say Brown and Gilligan. This is a time when a girl is still aware of what's happening. She can change things before her private self becomes completely buried.

Real feelings don't go away. Stuffing your real feelings can make you feel alone. The less real you are in relationships, say Brown and Gilligan, the more alone you feel, no matter how many people are around you.

When you aren't the real you, you lose touch with what you know is right and true. You lose your anchor. When that happens, you can't tell the difference between right and wrong, true and false, what you feel or don't feel. Being real may feel scary, say Brown and Gilligan, but finding the courage to be real is necessary for real relationships. Having a strong inner sense of who you are can help you decide right or wrong or lead you to answers. It's a lot like having a best friend inside you.

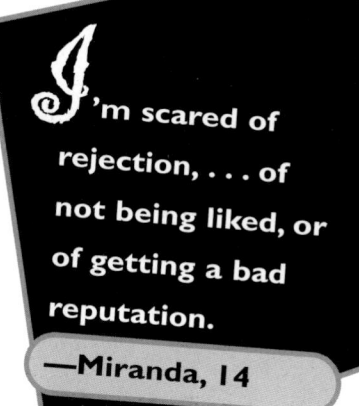

I'm scared of rejection, . . . of not being liked, or of getting a bad reputation.

—Miranda, 14

Conflict Resolution

Many girls have a parent who will listen and respect all the many moods a girl might go through. But as we talked about earlier, not every girl feels she gets listened to in her family. Then conflicts often arise.

Zerline, 18, of Washington, D.C., has a mom who is a conflict resolution mediator. "She helps you talk to someone when you have a disagreement," Zerline explains. Zerline's mom taught her some strategies for resolving conflicts in relationships.

Here are the basics:

- Identify the problem
- Focus on the problem
- Attack the problem, not the person
- Listen with an open mind
- Respect one another's feelings
- Take responsibility for your actions

We've begun to talk about some of these. Let's continue by identifying one specific problem many girls brought up: the problem of chores.

Identify and Focus on the Problem

"I know I have a lot of responsibilities," says Melissa, 12, from Texas, "but sometimes I'd rather be gardening or watering the plants outside instead of working inside."

Sound familiar? In many families, kids share in the chores. And there's not always agreement about who should do what! Here's a contrast in chores in two Hmong families. The families were interviewed by Ellen Tomson for an article that appeared in the *St. Paul Pioneer Press* in Minnesota.

Betty, 11, is a daughter in the first Hmong family. "On a typical Saturday, Betty washes and

Want to Fight about Clothes and Bedrooms?

*E*ver fight with a parent about what you wear or how your room looks? Although these are common battlegrounds, lots of girls have discovered it's silly to get too upset over clothes and bedrooms.

When people put the "small stuff" in perspective, finding guidelines everyone can live with gets easier. Maybe you can wear that outfit your mom hates if you just don't wear it to school. Everyone can give a little and gain a little—and save a lot of emotional energy for the important questions in life.

hangs five loads of laundry," wrote Tomson. "On a typical weekday, she washes the dishes that accumulated while she was at school; cooks rice in an electric pot on the counter; and watches over a wandering toddler while her brothers swarm through the kitchen playing. If there have been visitors, Betty needs no prompting to tidy up when they leave."

Pam has a different life. "My parents are a little bit more modern," she says, "and they don't really make me do chores that much unless I'm being punished or something. . . . They used to make me sweep and do the dishes and make rice before they came home and stuff. My brother usually didn't have to do anything. For some reason, I never really wondered why, but I knew that he didn't have to."

Some girls told me they do more chores simply because they are the oldest child. Nicole says, "My brother is six so he can't mow the lawn because he can't reach the handle. So he usually gets small chores like helping with the dishes or cleaning up his room. My sister and I have most of the outside chores like mowing the lawn and taking care of dusting inside and trimming the hedges outside."

Liliana, 12, from Texas, writes, "I have some problems with my brother. Sometimes I have to pick up for him and fold his clothes. My mom thinks I should do chores like sweeping, washing dishes, and cleaning the tables. I'd rather be outside gardening."

> *My* brother usually didn't have to do [chores]. . . . I never really wondered why.
>
> —Pam, 14

What's wrong with girls helping around the house? Again, nothing, except when gender bias enters in. Girls are more than good housekeepers or good baby-sitters. If a girl gets a message that keeping house and taking care of babies are the only things she can do, she may feel locked into a certain role.

Attack the Problem, Not the Parent

How does a girl stop herself from blowing up with anger, attacking a parent or someone else in the family who seems to be in the wrong? Anger is a normal human emotion. Some girls think that they're not supposed to be mad or have other bad feelings about their mom or dad, brother or sister. In a book called *I'm Not Mad, I Just Hate You!*, author Dr. Roni Cohen-Sandler writes that even when we're close to someone, we sometimes feel disappointed by them or believe we've been mistreated by them. Remembering that anger is normal is the first step in handling it.

Next, when you feel angry, ask yourself: What's troubling me? Do you want your parent to stop criticizing something about you? Do you wish they'd recognize an area where you're trying hard and you've made progress? Then, suggests Cohen-Sandler, try telling the person how you feel. Tell

Letting
It Out

I think the most frustrating thing about being a girl in a family might be that girls need other girls to talk to. Sometimes there may not be a girl or a woman around. . . . The way I try to handle this problem is to tell my problems anyway, because somebody is better than nobody. I have learned a whole lot from doing that. If you let a person know how you feel and talk to them about your problems, you have a greater chance of getting help.

—*Erica*, 12

your mom, "I feel hurt and insulted when you criticize my clothes." Or say to your dad, "I studied half an hour longer every day this semester to try to improve my grades. I wish you'd realize how hard school is for me." Statements like these will be easier for a parent to understand than the sound of a bedroom door slamming.

Listen with *an Open Mind*

There are many reasons behind what parents and families do! Take chores again for example. Some parents are trying to teach kids responsibility; others feel overwhelmed and need help. Betty, the Hmong girl with so many household duties, is being taught "to be a good daughter-in-law for her future husband's family," according to Ellen Tomson.

How does a girl go about seeing things from her family's point of view as well as staying true to her own view? It's not an easy task. Miranda, 14, describes how she used to communicate about problems in her family. "I got my mom and stepfather to listen by screaming and blaring my music," she says. "Eventually, they'd come in and say, 'What's the matter?' I'd break down and scream some more and then cry." It must have been clear that something was not okay, but Miranda and her family went through a lot of hard feelings before being able to communicate.

Grace, 11, who lives in Minnesota, sometimes finds it harder to speak and listen at school than at home. "I feel sometimes that I can't say anything— that's at school," she says. "I have to be a perfect little girl. But other times I push away the feeling and speak my mind. That's what I do the most." At home, Grace feels she can talk things over honestly with her mom. "It's not often that my mom doesn't listen to me," Grace says. "I really like that about my mom."

It's great if a girl is surrounded by good listeners. Sometimes the person she can talk to will be a father, brother, sister, teacher, friend, or someone else. *Who* doesn't matter. Being able to talk and listen openly does.

Respect One Another's *Feelings*

Grace, who lives with her mom, tells one story about how complex relationships can be. One morning, she'd had a really big fight with her mom. "I can be really crabby in the morning, so I get into fights with my mom a lot," Grace says. Then she got on the bus to go to school.

The school bus driver often talked to the students on his bus. That day, "he gave us a lecture about how homosexuality is a sin," Grace remembers. Grace and her mom have a different view about homosexuality—sexual feelings between people of the same gender—than the bus driver did. In fact, Grace's mom has a woman for a partner, not a man.

When Grace got home, she told her mom about the bus driver's comments. "We forgot our grudges and complained to my principal," says Grace. "We did a petition and won." The bus driver was transferred to a different bus.

Grace started out mad at her mom but forgot her anger when she and her mom joined together in a common cause. In this case, they were able to respect one another's feelings.

Lisa has tried to understand the reasons behind what she considers the sexist actions of her father. "He grew up in a male-oriented environment," she says. "Though he had two sisters, his family was such that his father was the absolute leader, no question. My father was subconsciously taught that girls were inferior and [that] he had to be the controller."

Eventually, Lisa's mom and dad got divorced. Lisa explains, "He treated my mother as if everything she did was wrong, no matter what she did or how she did it. My mom thought she was actually in the wrong, and she took the abuse for years. Finally, she noticed him doing it to me, and she saw that I really hadn't done anything wrong. That's when she decided to leave him."

After Lisa's dad was single again, he started dating. "He has learned a lot from some of the women he has dated," Lisa says. "He is much less

> *If your mom does not listen, ask her if you can have some private time with her.*
>
> —Erin, 9

overbearing toward me now. In fact, he is getting married this April to a woman who I think will be very helpful in making him realize that girls are every bit as good as boys." Lisa's ability to see a change in her dad shows a willingness on her part to listen openly.

Even though Lisa is listening openly and her dad is trying to change, that doesn't mean everything's perfect. "I am still afraid of him," Lisa admits. Being afraid yet still listening openly shows a lot of courage on Lisa's part.

Erin had a great suggestion that helped her speak, listen, and respect feelings. "If your mom does not listen," says Erin, "ask her if you can have some private time with her and talk to her about what's been happening, and she might listen to you. I had some private time with my mom, and she listened to what was happening. She understood the whole thing."

Take Responsibility
for Your Actions

How can you take responsibility for your own actions when a parent seems to be in control? Consider chores again, looking this time at inside versus outside chores. "The way I would handle it," says Melissa, "would be by doing both inside and outside chores."

Heather, 11, a girl from Virginia, wrote a letter to *American Girl* magazine with an idea. "Sometimes if I do a chore without being asked or do chores my parents don't expect, they give me more privileges. It's not fun, but it's worth doing chores to get more privileges."

Alicia, 13, suggests first doing the inside chore—like cleaning your room. She'd then point out to her parents the benefits to outside chores. In her case, that would be saying to her parents that if they let her do more outside chores, she might find cans, which she could sell to earn money.

No girl can control her parents or anyone else in her family. But she can control her own actions and attitudes. You can show your parents and others that you are being responsible with what Lynda Madaras, author of *My Feelings, My Self*, calls "I-messages." Compare these two statements:

- You make me so frustrated when you won't listen to why I'm upset.
- I feel so frustrated when I can't tell you why I'm upset.

See the difference? The first one blames the parent. The second one is an I-message. It says that you are a person with feelings and that you have a need to tell those feelings. You've taken responsibility for you.

Taking
the Long View

Sometimes problems in families are so big that no matter what you do, you can't seem to get your parents to listen to you. Many things can cause parents to stop being able to communicate with their children, including drug abuse, alcoholism, or mental illness. In that case, one thing you can do is think about how someday you might forgive them.

Then, in the meantime, focus on friends, other family members, and other adults for the attention and love you deserve. You might also attend a support group for youth and consider getting counseling. Never keep severe problems secret. Talk them over with an adult you trust.

A girl can control both what she *does* do and what she *does not* do. Zerline, the girl whose mother is a conflict resolution mediator, tells some things *not* to do in resolving conflicts. Do not name call, sneer, get even, hit; boss others, not take responsibility, make excuses; bring up the past, blame, not listen, make threats. By keeping your own actions on track, trying to do what's fair and trying not to do what's unfair, you've taken a giant step toward being responsible for your actions— and for yourself.

chapter four

Where Can a Girl Go?

> My mom will not let me go places after
> dark or let me just hang out somewhere.
>
> —*Miranda*, 14

You may have noticed that, as girls become teenagers, parents often begin to fear more and more for their safety. Parents' fears may lead them to try to shelter girls. That's what happened to Erin. "When we lived in Ohio, we were in a very dangerous neighborhood," says Erin. "So we could only play in our backyard."

Nicole says, "My mom thinks the outside world is dangerous not just for girls but for all three of us—my sister, my brother, and me. There's a lot more violence and stuff. . . . So my mom's kind of overprotective."

Alicia writes, "If I go to the mall, an adult needs to go with me. My parents think that something will happen to me."

Chiori Santiago, a writer for a family magazine, contrasted the situation for boys. "As teenagers, boys earn more freedom and privileges; girls become more cloistered. Boys cruise around at night; girls must stay home. Boys take the bus alone; girls must not. Boys are taught to face the world with courage; girls are taught to view it with fear."

My mom's kind of overprotective.

—Nicole, 11

What do you think? Is the world dangerous? A few years ago, the Center for Women Policy Studies (CWPS) surveyed girls about their thoughts about violence. CWPS received nearly 500 responses. A majority of the girls reported that they had seen acts of violence. Many girls said they'd been in fights. Nearly half the girls felt that girls can be just as violent as boys can be.

How It Feels

How does it feel when your parents are afraid for you? Katy, 12, a girl from New Hampshire, wrote to *American Girl* with this story. "One time a friend invited me to go to a roller-skating rink with her. My mother wouldn't let me go. She had never met the girl or her parents, and the rink was in a

Friends

*I*t scares me all the pressures on girls today. It seems like it's so much harder for girls than it is for guys. It's almost a man's world. The friendships I build are promising to me. That's . . . one of the most important things . . . just being able to know I have friends.

—*Pam, 14*

town she wasn't familiar with. At the time, I felt like I was just being treated like a baby."

Kasie writes, "My parents (especially my dad) think that I am so helpless in this world. They think I have no idea as to what I am supposed to do if I do get into trouble . . . so they try and isolate me. That just makes me rebellious and mad!"

Pam also had a vivid description of her feelings. "I'm like this little princess locked up in this castle, and I can't get out," she says. Maybe Gao feels trapped as well when she says, "My parents don't give me a lot of options. They just want me to stay home."

Of course, it feels good sometimes to be protected by your parents! "I think I should be protected by my mom," says Erin, "because if I got in a lot of trouble, I would need help from somebody, and my mom would be protecting me."

"I am very scared when I hear the news. . . . Many people die every day because of gangs shooting students at their school," writes Liliana. Nicole says her mom doesn't want her to take care of herself, but "I know that I could take care of myself if I tried to."

Kasie feels the same way. Her parents have shifted their attitudes. "I can take care of myself, and I think they are starting to realize that I can," she writes. "They just don't want to let me go." Kasie's comment shows her ability to step over to her parents' viewpoint, a sign of her growing maturity. Although her parents don't want to lose Kasie as their "little girl," that doesn't mean Kasie will stop growing up—or could, even if she tried.

Melanie, 12, a girl from Texas,

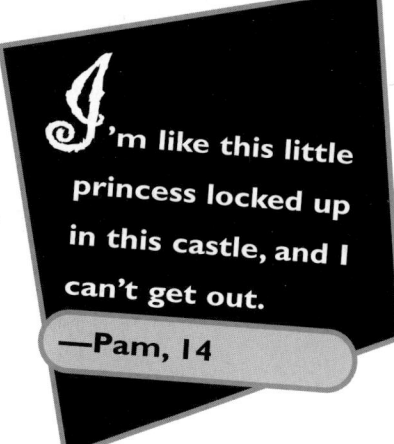

I'm like this little princess locked up in this castle, and I can't get out.

—Pam, 14

focuses on her own reactions, rather than on her mom's. "It used to be that when my mom said no [to going to the mall without an adult], I'd get upset and pout. Now I see she just doesn't want anything to happen to me."

Some Strategies

It's a fact that the world can be a dangerous place. But it's a fiction that girls can't learn to take care of themselves as well as anyone else. Besides, this world is the only one we have. If a girl doesn't learn to navigate it, no matter how dangerous it is, she may feel scared and helpless.

So what do girls do when they want to explore? Pam approached her parents this way. "I said, 'You want me to survive [but] how am I ever going to if you trap me in the house all the time? . . . If you want me to grow up and learn how to live in this world, you're going to have to let me experience it.'"

Some parents might agree. But Pam's parents weren't swayed by that argument. Pam's reasoning—

> One time a friend invited me to go to a roller-skating rink with her. My mother wouldn't let me go. . . . I felt like I was just being treated like a baby.
>
> —Katy, 12

Ready, Set, Talk

Here are some more tips for approaching your family with an important issue—it may be a conflict you want to resolve or it may be a new responsibility you'd like to have. The tips are based on ideas in *I'm Not Mad, I Just Hate You!*

- Choose which issues are most important to you; don't sweat the small stuff!
- Plan ahead what you're going to say.
- Say it at a time when you're feeling calm, not upset.
- Stick to the subject of what you want and how you feel.
- Let the other person talk, too.
- Be prepared to compromise.
- If you and your parent can't agree, take a break for an hour, a day, a week to consider alternative solutions.
- Try again.
- If you and your parent still can't agree, be proud that you handled the situation well.

that she needed to know how to handle the outside world—made sense, yet her parents fears remained.

Nicole says that a girl who has done baby-sitting has shown evidence that she can take care of herself while taking care of other people. "I stay home alone for hours at a time," she continues. "That's also evidence." Nicole used these examples when trying to convince her mom to let her ride the bus alone.

Alicia says she demonstrates that she can handle herself by "not hanging around with the wrong crowd." She has a point. If your parents believe you show good judgment about the people you trust, they'll find it easier to trust you.

Pam shows her good judgment this way: "When I go places," she says, "I go in groups so that I'm not by myself."

Pam echoes the girls in the CWPS survey. They named three top ways of protecting themselves: learn self-defense, tell someone (if you encounter a dangerous situation), always go places with a friend. Pam's approach is a good plan. Saying what you feel and listening to how your parents feel is another good plan.

One mother and daughter decided that developing physical strength was one key to safety. The daughter got involved in a number of activities to build confidence and strength. For example, she spent three weeks camping and hiking in the mountains of Montana with a YWCA group. The experience helped her grow physically stronger. But it also helped her get to know herself, her thoughts, her inner strengths. "You know what you're made of," as Mary, the mother, put it. "Even though you still may have moments when you may trip up, you know how strong you can feel."

In the best of worlds, no parent and no girl would be afraid. We wouldn't even have to have this discussion! We don't have that world. But we

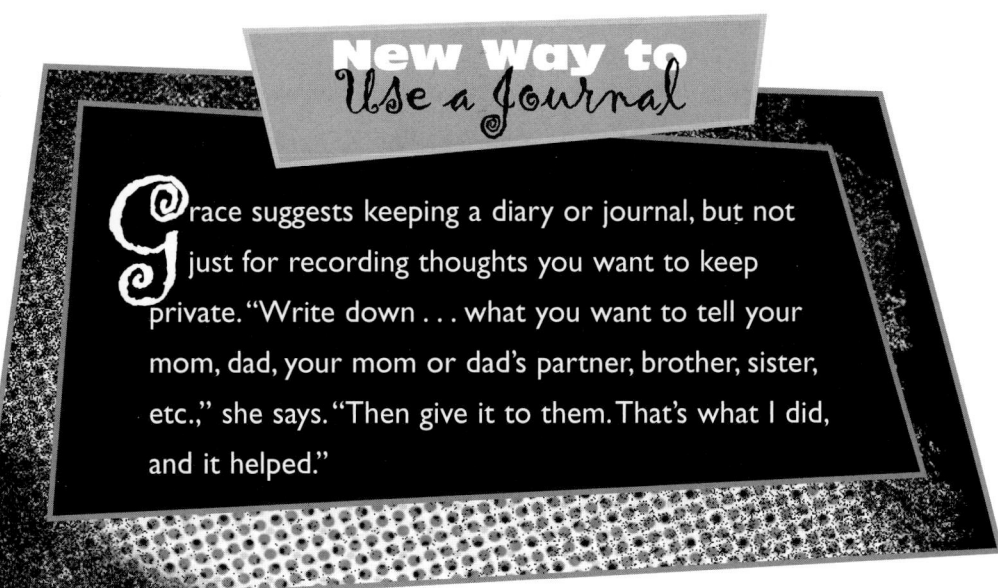

New Way to Use a Journal

Grace suggests keeping a diary or journal, but not just for recording thoughts you want to keep private. "Write down . . . what you want to tell your mom, dad, your mom or dad's partner, brother, sister, etc.," she says. "Then give it to them. That's what I did, and it helped."

can work toward a world where everyone is treated with respect. You help by staying true to your talents, your hopes, and your dreams. And the truth is, if the world is in such a sorry state, it needs all of us—girls and boys, women and men— and our passion for change and for what is right to make a better world.

Not Overnight

Don't be hard on yourself if it takes a while to figure things out with your family. You may find that you have to find your own way through.

Lots of girls told me they give their parents some time, too.

> Relationships based on trust, communication, and positive things are definitely a better direction to follow.
>
> —Jessica, 16

Jessica says, "I handled the situations [with my family] the best way I knew how, which wasn't the best way at all. I would scream my reactions out, then try to get my own way by saying everything I could, trying to get them to change their minds about something they wouldn't let me do. Sometimes I would say things to deliberately hurt them, then of course regret it after the act was done.

"I've . . . learned that saying hurtful things and being selfish and stubborn not only made the situation turn worse fast but also started to make my relationship with my parents slowly turn into one based on negative things. Now I realize that relationships based on trust, communication, and positive things are definitely a better direction to follow in life."

chapter five

Whose Body Is This?

My family wants me to look nice. What they think is nice is not nice to me.

— *Lupita*, 13

Body image—how you view your body—is an important part of how a girl views herself. Your view of your body can be affected by messages from your culture and from your family. A girl also needs privacy in her family and control over her own body.

A recent national survey of teenage girls in North America found that girls lose a lot of confidence between the ages of thirteen and sixteen. Marion Woodman and Elinor Dickson say in their book *Dancing in the Flames* that this happens because girls don't have enough good role models. Instead of looking to older girls and women as examples, girls look to fashion magazines. There, "they see the kinds of bodies and faces that they themselves can never have," wrote Woodman and Dickson. "[Yet] these are the ideals that are held up for them if they want to be successful, particularly with men."

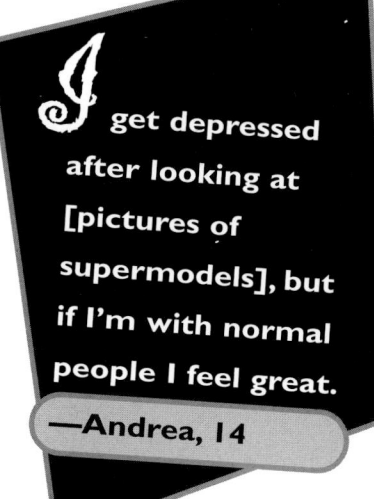

I get depressed after looking at [pictures of supermodels], but if I'm with normal people I feel great.

—Andrea, 14

Mixed Messages

Writer Anastasia Higginbotham looked at several months' worth of teen magazines to study the messages for girls. In an article in *Ms.* magazine, Higginbotham described the messages as contradictory. "Be pretty, but not so pretty that you intimidate boys," was one message. Being "too pretty" can attract the wrong kind of boyfriend. It can also threaten other girls, fathers, teachers, and bosses. "Be smart but not so smart" and "be athletic but not so athletic" were similar mixed messages.

Mary Pipher points out the problem with these mixed messages. "While the rules for proper female behavior aren't clearly stated, the punishment for breaking them is harsh." Pipher says girls who "break the rules" are sometimes scorned, criticized, and teased.

The push to look like the models in magazines can lead to self-destructive behaviors. Two dangerous eating disorders are anorexia and bulimia. A girl with anorexia starves herself. One with bulimia binges on food, then purges it by throwing up or taking laxatives. Girls with these disorders can become severely ill or even die. If you suspect that you have an eating disorder or that a friend does, get help right away.

Most girls have a less extreme reaction to the pressure to be pretty and thin. "I don't think it's wrong," writes Miranda. Nicole says, "I sort of think it's wrong to pressure girls to look sexy, but if I had the choice, I probably would look like that. But my mom doesn't let me. The style of showing part of your stomach—she doesn't let me wear that kind of stuff."

Erin offered some ideas about how to make changes in teen magazines and ads. "I don't like those ads that make girls look sexy," she says. "I would hate to do

> *It's wrong to pressure girls to look sexy, but if I had the choice, I probably would look like that. But my mom doesn't let me.*
>
> —Nicole, 11

that—make my body wear all that junk. To fight it, you could go to the place where those people work or send them a letter and tell them they should not [present] kids that age that way."

What Parents *Say*

Remember how so many more black girls than white girls look to their mothers and grand-mothers as examples of beauty? Any girl can look to her family as a strong defense against the unhealthy effect of media messages.

One thing girls can do is to listen to and absorb the praise parents give them about qualities other than looks. Studies have shown that parents who praise a daughter for her actions, rather than for her looks, actually strengthen her body image. If a girl is great at math, or throws a mean curve ball, or is patient with younger kids, those are all good qualities. If your family helps you focus on your good qualities, that's your best defense against eating disorders or just feeling low about your looks.

> *Parents who praise a daughter for her actions, rather than for her looks, actually strengthen her body image.*

But families don't always realize the heavy burden girls carry regarding looks. And a parent may not realize he or she can play a role in helping a girl stay confident and proud.

Here's the message Alicia gets and how she responds. "My family expects me to look pretty and fix my hair up," she says. "My brother likes to tease me because of the way I dress. I get them to stop when I say, 'No one runs my life.' I tell them that no one should tell me how to dress."

"My parents think I'm too skinny," says Pam. "They think I should be not fat, just a little larger. They think it's more wholesome." Gao says, "I'm always scared of getting too much overweight. My parents want me to be really big. They think that's nicer and better for girls."

Nicole finds that her family doesn't pressure her "because they think I'm really pretty." But her dad does get mad at her sister over looks. "She likes to shave her head, doesn't care what she wears, doesn't care what people say. My dad doesn't really like that. . . . He sort of expects her to be more like a girl than a boy. But he doesn't care what I do, because he knows that I would never shave my head. And I always care what I wear."

Erin also had some pretty strong ideas about how to deal with her family expecting her to look a certain way. "My brother and sister call me a boy because I have hardly any hair. . . . I tell my mom and they get in trouble, or I just ignore it."

Developing *You*

For many girls, getting their period is a time when they feel differently about their bodies and themselves. "I have started my period, and at first I thought I was so mature," writes Kasie. "But now it's just a course in life. The way I feel when I have my period is so terrible. . . . I feel crampy and sick, but I am growing up."

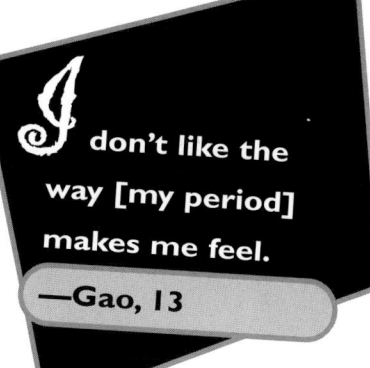

I don't like the way [my period] makes me feel.

—Gao, 13

Gao notices the mood swings some girls experience with their monthly cycle. "I don't like the way [my period] makes me feel," she says. "It's annoying. People in your family get on your nerves easily then. Sometimes they get on your nerves so much you just blow up. Then it's kind of hard, because you never meant it."

A girl's family—often but not always a mom—can make a big difference in how the girl feels about menstruation. "My mom ignores it," writes Liliana. "Sometimes my sister helps me a lot and tells me what to do."

"My sister told me everything," says Marie, 14. "I was twelve when I started, and my mom hadn't told me anything. My sister, who is older, told me about pads and tampons, what to do and what not to do."

"My mom, she knows it's going to happen sooner or later," says Pam. "So when it happens she doesn't really care. It kind of scares my dad. . . . If I'm on my period, I'm old enough to make him a grandfather. That sort of makes him uncomfortable because in a way he doesn't want me to grow up. He always wants me to be a little girl."

Your Space, Your Body

Privacy becomes especially important to many girls as their bodies develop. Sometimes total privacy isn't possible. You may share a room with a sister. Or maybe people in the family are used to coming into your room whenever they like. If you need more privacy, do bring it up. Point out that you're not a little girl anymore and that, as a young woman, you need privacy. Your parents can work with you to explain this to brothers and sisters. Some families make a new house rule regarding privacy as girls grow older.

Here's what Nicole, who shares a room with her sister, does about privacy. "I shut myself in my room and read or listen to music," she says. "Or I play with my cat. If my sister is in my room, I ask

What Is Abuse?

If someone treats you in ways that hurt you physically or that make you feel afraid or ashamed, that's abuse. There are three kinds of abuse—physical, emotional, and sexual abuse.

- Physical abuse involves any violent action such as hitting or pushing or slapping. A threat of physical violence is also physical abuse.
- Examples of emotional abuse include someone putting you down, calling you names, ignoring you, or refusing to talk to you.
- Sexual abuse happens whenever a girl is pressured to do sexual things she doesn't want to do.

All these kinds of abuse are wrong. Some of these actions are against the law. If you suspect you are being abused, tell an adult you trust.

my mom if I can go in my mom's room." Some girls ask to have their own phone. A girl who shares a bedroom can take a cordless phone into another room to find privacy for talking with friends.

Sometimes the problem of privacy is much bigger than a girl not having a bedroom to herself. In some families, personal boundaries are ignored. A father, stepfather, uncle, older brother, or another person may view a girl's body as belonging to themselves rather than to her. This can result in sexual abuse. Sexual abuse may include touching a girl in ways a father or a brother or any relative should not touch, like touching the breasts or bottom or another private place. Being hugged in a way that feels wrong or having to hear words of a sexual nature can also be sexually abusive.

If something like this is happening to you or someone you know, seek help. A good hotline to call is 1-800-799-SAFE—also known as the National Domestic Violence Hotline—run by the Council on Family Violence.

Every girl has the right to her own body. No one has the right to touch a girl without her consent. A family member who abuses a girl sexually may try to frighten her and blame her. Never keep a secret that feels scary or wrong. And remember that when sexual abuse happens, it is never, under any circumstances, the girl's fault.

chapter six

Ordinary Courage in a New World

> At adolescence, girls' ordinary courage—girls' seemingly effortless ability... to speak their mind... tends to turn into something heroic.
>
> —Lyn Mikel Brown and Carol Gilligan

As many girls become teenagers, saying what they feel and think often means great risk. Girls risk "losing their relationships and finding themselves powerless and alone," as Brown and Gilligan put it.

Girls face a different world from the one in which their parents grew up. In some ways, ours is a more dangerous world. There are more drugs, more violence. But in other, wonderful ways, this is a more exciting world. Girls have more opportunities than ever before.

Your Wise Woman
Project

ave you ever admired the wisdom of your mom, aunt, grandmother, great-grandmother, a neighbor, or any other woman? Have you wished she would tell you more about how she grew up and what she knows? One idea is to make a book that records the wisdom of the woman you admire. The Girl Scouts' website at www.gsusa.org offers tips on how to approach her, what questions to ask, how to record information, how to make a scrapbook, and more.

Another website—called Girl Zone at www.girlzone.com—published an article called "Use Their Wisdom to Bloom into the Woman You Want to Become." The author, Cinse Bonino, suggested adding your own wisdom to the end of your homemade book. Then give a copy to the woman you admire. (You might be surprised how much she will appreciate it!) Keep one copy for yourself. Then you can turn to it when the going gets rough or whenever you'd like to connect with your wise woman.

Parents may be uncertain, not knowing how best to prepare their daughters for this different world. Parents often want to give their daughters all they can—including freedom—yet at the same time they worry about keeping girls safe. Some parents worry about how to tell the truth to their daughters. Would telling a girl the "hard facts of life" scare her too much? The whole process can become quite complicated.

> *In a way [my dad] doesn't want me to grow up. He always wants me to be a little girl.*
> —Pam, 14

Judy Mann writes about her twelve-year-old daughter, who told Mann she thought women aren't always treated equally with men. Mann wondered how she should answer. Carol Gilligan suggested Mann answer this way: "Tell her she's right; things are not all that great for women. But [also tell her] that together, you and she will make a difference."

The You in Your Family

Your family launches you into a world that is so different from the one your parents knew when they grew up. How you face it can have a lot to do with your relationship with your family.

It's important that a family try to understand what a girl is up against and try to find ways to support her.

Sometimes this isn't possible. Not all families listen. If this is the case for you, remember the situation is not your fault. Don't blame yourself if you don't get the support you know you deserve. Instead, arm yourself with knowledge, and you

Oh, Brothers

Melissa's older brother often picks on her. Sometimes it seems to her that, although she's complained to her parents over and over about this, they don't seem to listen. "It's not like my parents don't care," writes Melissa. "It's just because they get tired of hearing the same things over and over again." It never hurts to recognize that parents sometimes get discouraged and quit thinking about how to solve any given problem.

can achieve as much as anyone. As more and more people pay attention to the lives of girls, more and more support will be available to you—from parents or teachers or a neighbor or books like this one.

Practice, Practice, Practice

So much of what you learn about yourself and your family will take practice. Practice listening to others. Practice hearing the thoughts of your private self. Practice looking at yourself, noticing all the things that make you who you are. Remember you cannot be summed up by words such as *sugar and spice and everything nice.* It may take time to change the way a parent sees a daughter or the way a daughter sees herself. But in the end, you'll find the effort is worth it.

By being honest and by having the courage to be all you can be, you build true, strong

> *The* best thing is to try and try again to have your parents listen to you. If you can't face your own feelings, just sit down with yourself and think the situation through. It really works.
>
> —Grace, 11

relationships with your family, with others, and with yourself. In good times and in bad, through conflicts and loving moments, you can always turn to the inner self you are nurturing, finding your own path to becoming the woman you choose to be.

Resources *for Girls*

If you want to learn more about your family, yourself, and the issues you're facing as you grow up, many publications, organizations, and programs have good information.

However, if you are facing a serious problem—such as physical or sexual abuse, harassment problems, depression, problems with drugs or alcohol, being pregnant, or running away from home—you can call 1-800-4-A-CHILD. You can also look in the yellow pages of your local telephone book under "Crisis Intervention." Phone numbers with an 800 or 888 area code are toll free. Remember, too, you can talk to a parent, an older sibling, an older friend, a school counselor, a teacher, or a religious leader.

Organizations—Mentors and Girl Groups

Volunteers at Big Sisters spend time with and mentor girls. Some chapters offer a Life Choices program that helps girls make the best decisions for themselves. You can also look in your phone book for a local Big Brothers Big Sisters number.

> Big Brothers Big Sisters of America
> 230 North 13th Street
> Philadelphia, PA 19107
> (215) 567-7000
> www.bbbsa.org

Girls, Incorporated has many local chapters where girls gather for fun and learning. The organization offers a program called Friendly PEERsuasion, in which girls help others resist drugs and alcohol, and has other activities that concern health, relationships, career planning, and sexuality.

> Girls, Incorporated
> 30 East 33rd Street
> New York, NY 10016
> (212) 689-3700
> www.girlsinc.org

Girl Scouts go way beyond camping these days and offer lots of fun learning experiences. A contemporary issues program helps girls learn about self-esteem, health issues, good relationships, stress management, and other topics. The national office can help you find a local troop.

Girl Scouts of the USA
420 Fifth Avenue
New York, NY 10018-2702
(800) 223-0624
www.gsusa.org

After-school YWCA clubs include PACT, a peer education program in which girls learn to teach other girls about health and sexuality issues, about how to resist peer pressure, and about how to be a leader.

YWCA of the USA
726 Broadway
New York, NY 10003
(800) YWCA-US1
www.ywca.org

Organizations—Health, Sexuality, and Body Changes

The National Eating Disorders Organization (NEDO) offers free information about anorexia, bulimia, and exercise addiction and makes local referrals for treatment.

NEDO
6655 South Yale Avenue
Tulsa, OK 74136
(918) 481-4044
www.laureate.com

If you have questions about homosexuality, you can contact the National Gay and Lesbian Task Force (NGLTF) for a referral to a local support group or organization for lesbian, gay, bisexual, and transgender young people.

NGLTF
1700 Kalorama Road NW
Washington, DC 20009
(202) 332-6483
www.ngltf.org

Planned Parenthood helps with questions about birth control, pregnancy tests, abortion, and sexuality counseling. They can send information. Dialing (800) 230-PLAN automatically connects you with the nearest clinic. Some areas offer a peer education service for girls.

Planned Parenthood Federation of America
810 Seventh Avenue
New York, NY 10019
(800) 829-7732
www.plannedparenthood.org

The Sex Information Education Councils will refer you to local organizations that can help with questions about the body, sex, and pregnancy.

Sex Information Education Councils of the United States
130 West 42nd Street, Suite 350
New York, NY 10036
(212) 819-9770
www.siecus.org

Magazines and Newspapers

Blue Jean, a magazine for older girls, focuses on publishing what young women are "thinking, saying, and doing."

> *Blue Jean*
> Post Office Box 507
> Victor, NY 14564
> (716) 924-4080
> www.bluejeanmag.com

New Girl Times is a national newspaper for girls. It has "all the news that's fit to empower."

> *New Girl Times*
> 215 West 84th Street
> New York, NY 10024
> (800) 560-7525

New Moon is a bimonthly magazine that has news and fiction for and about girls. *New Moon* is planned by an editorial board of girls aged nine to fourteen and has lots of things written and drawn by girls.

> *New Moon: The Magazine for Girls and Their Dreams*
> Post Office Box 3587
> Duluth, MN 55803
> (800) 381-4743
> www.newmoon.org

Teen Voices is a quarterly magazine written by teen girls about lots of good topics including body image, media stereotyping of girls, racism, sexual abuse, and family relationships. Most issues include fiction and poetry, too.

> *Teen Voices*
> Post Office Box 120027
> Boston, MA 02112-0027
> (800) 882-TEEN
> www.teen voices.com

YO!, a quarterly newspaper, is not just for girls, but it has plenty of writing by girls on a wide range of topics important to teens.

> *YO!*
> 450 Mission Street, Suite 204
> San Francisco, CA 94105
> (415) 243-4364

Websites

FeMiNa—-at www.femina.com—has a section for girls that includes information on books, careers, games, health, sports, music, technology programs, and links to girls' homepages.

Girl Power—at www.health.org/gpower—has all kinds of sub-categories, including a new one on body image, to go along with information on eating right, staying active, and respecting your body.

GirlTech—at www.girltech.com—encourages girls to explore the world of technology. Subcategories include a bulletin board, tech trips, girl views, cool games, and girls in sports.

Girl Zone—at www.girlzone.com—is governed by a teen advisory board and shares information on books, health, and self-image.

Troom—at www.troom.com—offers information on travel, music, issues, and body changes.

Girl Power

Books

Abner, Allison, and Linda Villarosa. *Finding Our Way: The Teen Girls' Survival Guide.* New York: HarperPerennial, 1996.

Cohen-Sandler, Roni and Michelle Silver. *I'm Not Mad I Just Hate You!: A New Understanding of Mother-Daughter Conflict.* New York: Viking, 1999.

Driscoll, Anne. *Girl to Girl: The Real Deal on Being a Girl Today.* Rockport, MA: Element, 1999.

Harlan, Judith. *Girl Talk: Staying Strong, Feeling Good, Sticking Together.* New York: Walker, 1997.

Jukes, Mavis. *It's a Girl Thing: How to Stay Healthy, Safe, and in Charge.* New York: Knopf, 1996.

McCoy, Kathy, and Charles Wibbelsman. *The Teenage Body Book.* New York: Putnam, 1999.

Roehm, Michelle, ed. *Girls Know Best: Advice for Girls from Girls on Just About Everything.* Hillsboro, OR: Beyond Words, 1997.

Sandler. Sara. *Ophelia Speaks: Adolescent Girls Write about Their Search for Self.* New York: HarperCollins, 1999.

Resources
for Parents and Teachers

Organizations

The catalog of the American Association of University Women (AAUW) lists publications and videos that encourage girls in nontraditional areas and that give advice on handling issues such as sexual harassment. AAUW also sponsors Sister-to-Sister girls' conferences around the country.

> AAUW
> 1111 16th Street NW
> Washington, DC 20036
> (202) 785-7700
> (call (800) 326-AAUW for catalog)
> www.aauw.org

Girls, Incorporated provides a variety of resources to teachers and parents to promote girls' self-confidence.

> Girls, Incorporated
> 30 East 33rd Street
> New York, NY 10016
> (212) 689-3700
> www.girlsinc.org

The Melpomene Institute, which addresses women's and girl's health needs, will send information packets on how adults affect girls' body images.

> The Melpomene Institute
> 1010 University Avenue
> St. Paul, MN 55104
> (651) 642-1951
> www.melpomene.org

The National Women's History Project has plenty of information and resources about our foremothers. The organization offers a catalog and has a website.

> National Women's History Project
> 7738 Bell Road
> Windsor, CA 95492
> (707) 838-6000
> www.nwhp.org

The Women's College Coalition has a website—called Expect the Best from a Girl—for resources and tips on helping girls get the most out of school and life.

> Women's College Coalition
> 125 Michigan Avenue NE
> Washington, DC 20017
> (202) 234-0443
> www.academic.org

The Women's Educational Equity Act (WEEA) will send a free catalog with plenty of resources to promote girls' self-esteem.

> WEEA
> Equity Resource Center
> EDC 55 Chapel Street
> Newton, MA 02158-1060
> (800) 225-3088
> www.edc.org/womensequity

Books

Bingham, Mindy. *Things Will Be Different for My Daughter: A Practical Guide to Building Her Self-Esteem and Self-Reliance.* New York: Penguin, 1995.

Brown, Lyn Mikel and Carol Gilligan. *Meeting at the Crossroads: Women's Psychology and Girls' Development.* New York: Ballantine, 1993.

Eagle, Carol. *All That She Can Be: Helping Your Daughter Achieve Her Full Potential and Maintain Her Self-Esteem during the Critical Years of Adolescence.* New York: Simon & Schuster, 1993.

Gadeberg, Jeanette. *Brave New Girls: Creative Ideas to Help Girls Be Confident, Healthy, and Happy.* Minneapolis, MN: Fairview Press, 1997.

Maccoby, Eleanor E. *The Two Sexes: Growing Up Apart, Coming Together.* Cambridge, MA: Belknap Press, 2000.

Mann, Judy. *The Difference: Discovering the Hidden Ways We Silence Girls—Finding Alternatives That Can Give Them a Voice.* New York: Warner, 1996.

Odean, Kathleen. *Great Books for Girls: More Than 600 Books to Inspire Today's Girls and Tomorrow's Women.* New York: Ballantine, 1997.

Orenstein, Peggy. *SchoolGirls: Young Women, Self-Esteem, and the Confidence Gap.* New York: Bantam Doubleday, 1995.

Pipher, Mary. *Reviving Ophelia: Saving the Selves of Adolescent Girls.* New York: Ballantine, 1995.

Girl Power

Index

About *the Author*

Karen Lound, an award-winning fiction writer, holds an MFA in creative writing from the University of Alabama and has taught creative writing at both the high school and college levels. In addition, she frequently writes on nonfiction topics such as education and women's issues for newspapers and magazines. Her first book, also published by Lerner Publications Company, was *AIDS: Examining the Crisis.* Lound lives in Minneapolis, Minnesota.